Teenie Weenie in a Too Big World

Margot Sunderland

Illustrated by

Nicky Armstrong

Speechmark

Speechmark Publishing Ltd
Telford Road, Bicester, Oxon OX26 4LQ, UK
www.speechmark.net

One day, Teenie Weenie was walking along . . .

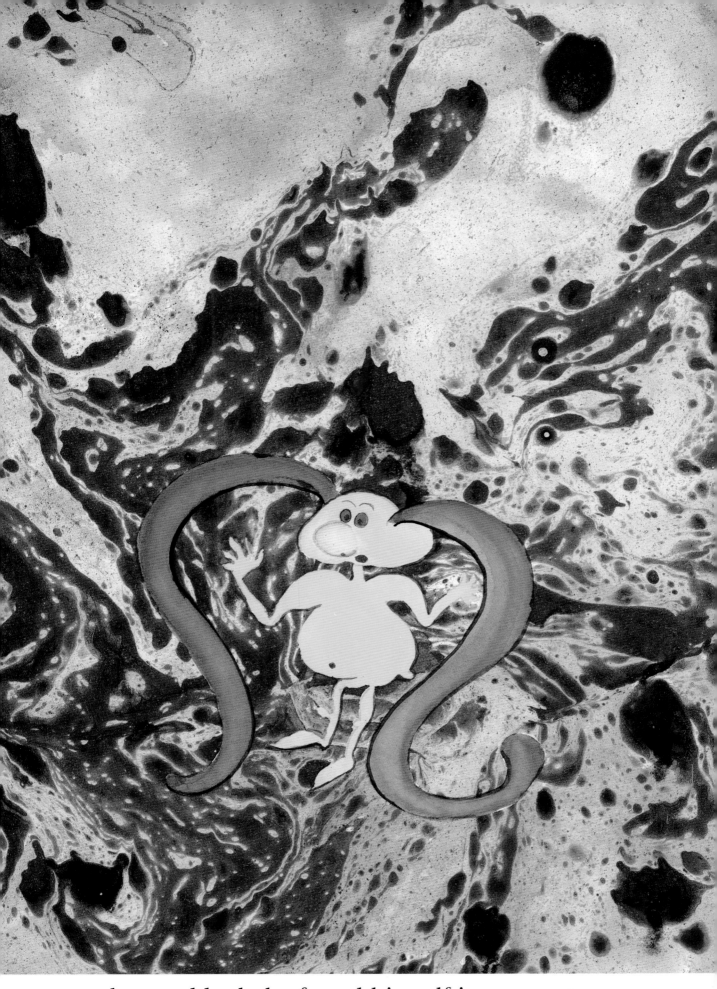

. . . when suddenly he found himself in a scrumbly, screechy place.

It was full of noises and crashes and humpy bumpy things . . .

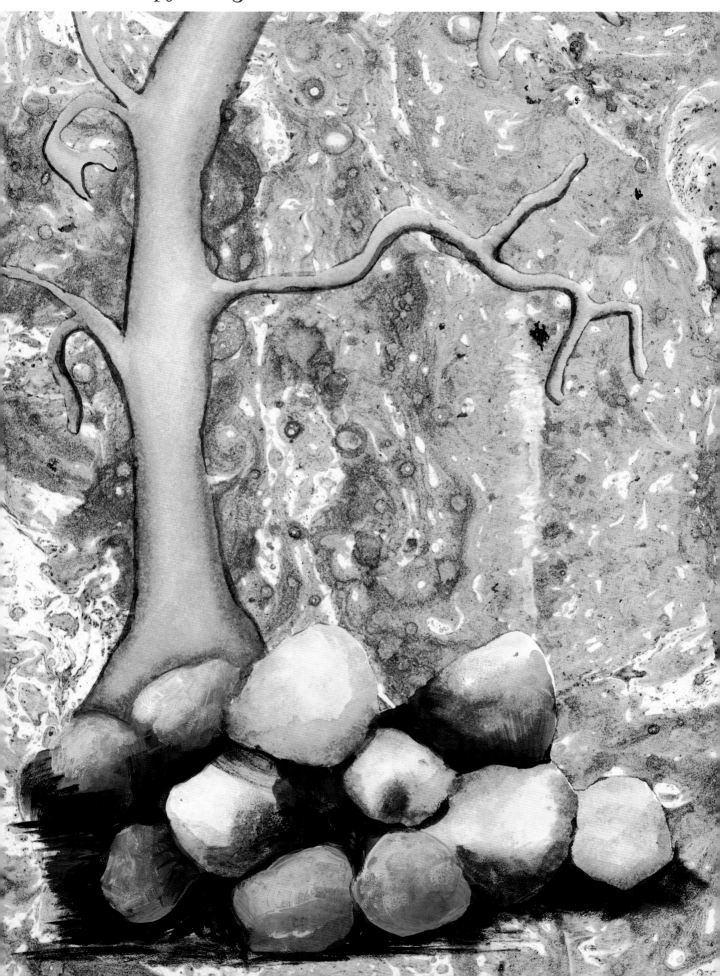

. . . and things that swooped and scratched.

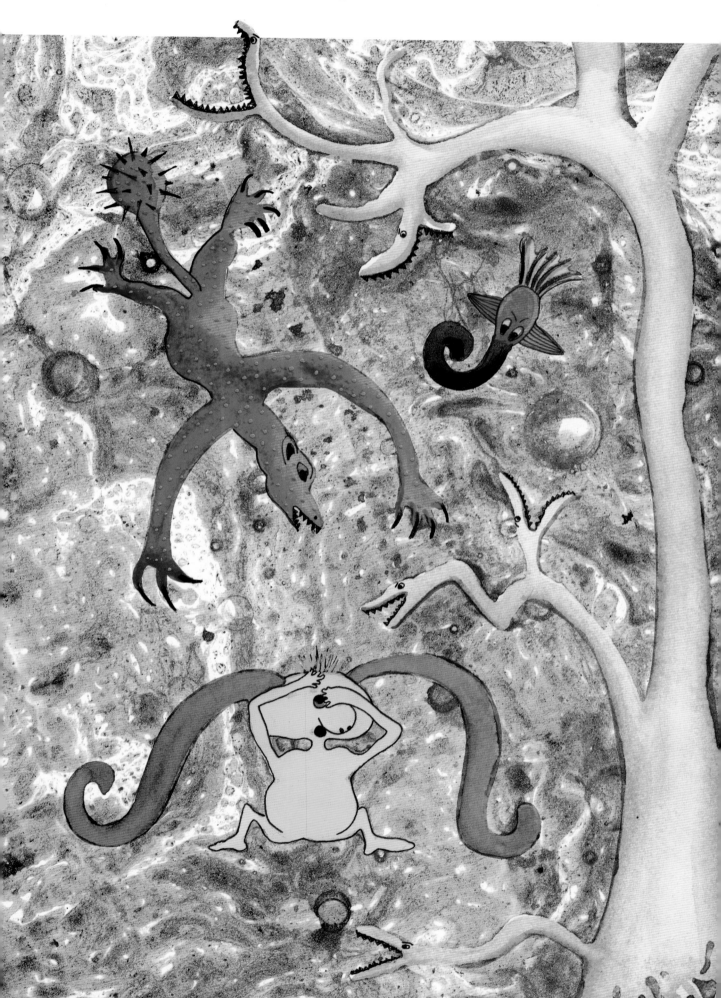

Then a Snarling Snippercracker snapped at Teenie Weenie. Teenie Weenie cowered.

He walked along a bit more, and a big, banging branch whacked into him. Teenie Weenie felt even smaller.

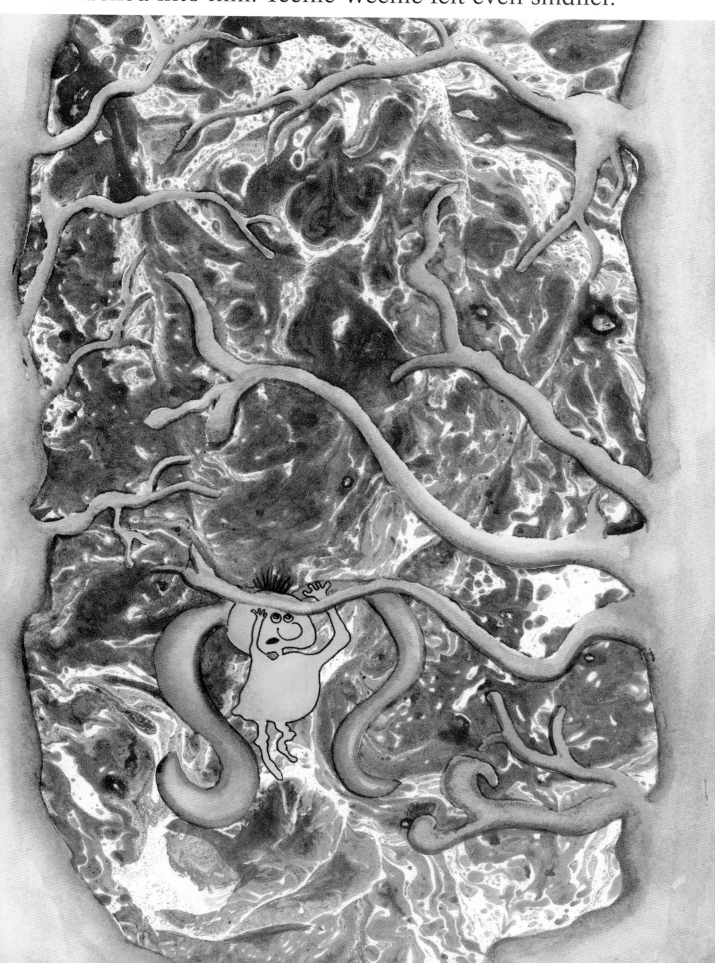

Then he fell into a jangly, tangly mess, right there by the water's edge.

And the more Teenie Weenie found the scrumbly, screechy place too hard, the smaller he felt.

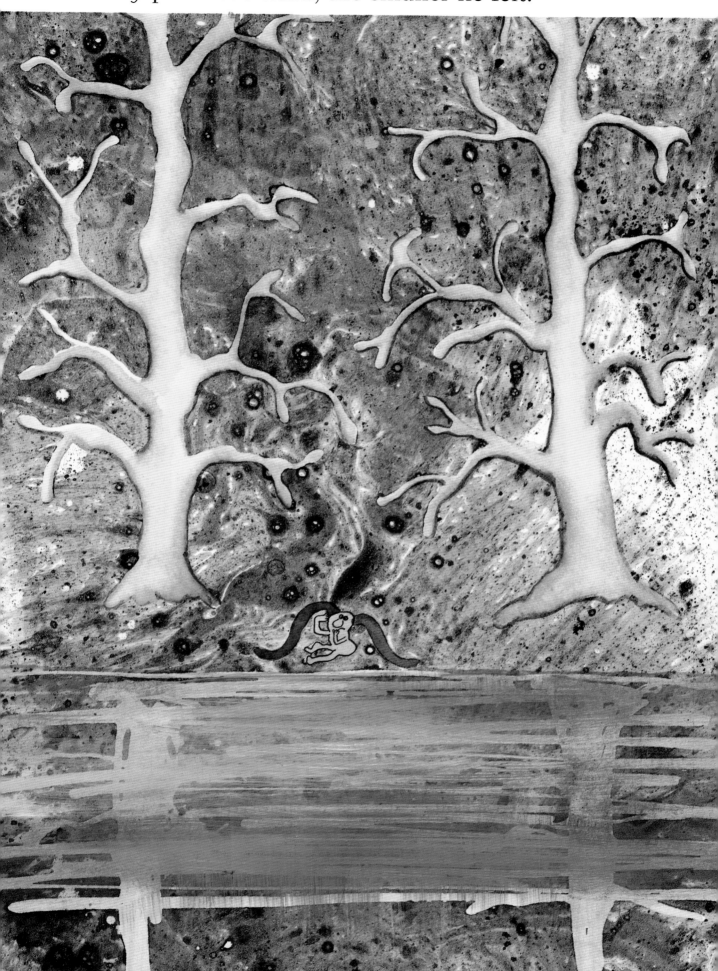

And by the time all manner of creatures
had snarled, sneered and squawked at him . . .

. . . and by the time all manner of wild winds
had blown at him, and stinging rain had battered
him blue, he felt he was little more than a speck.

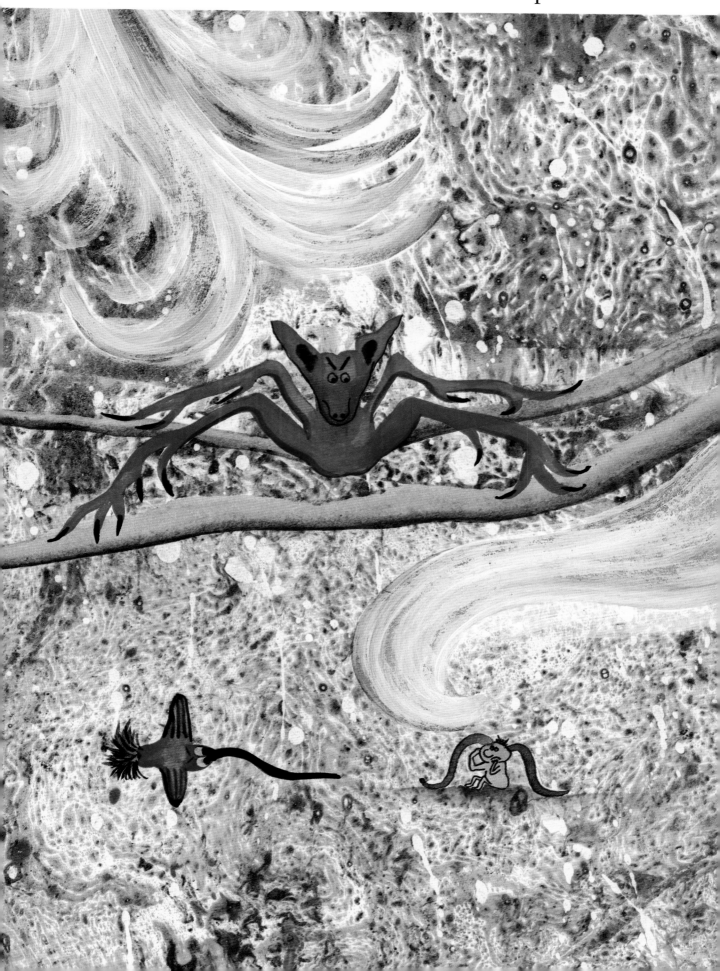

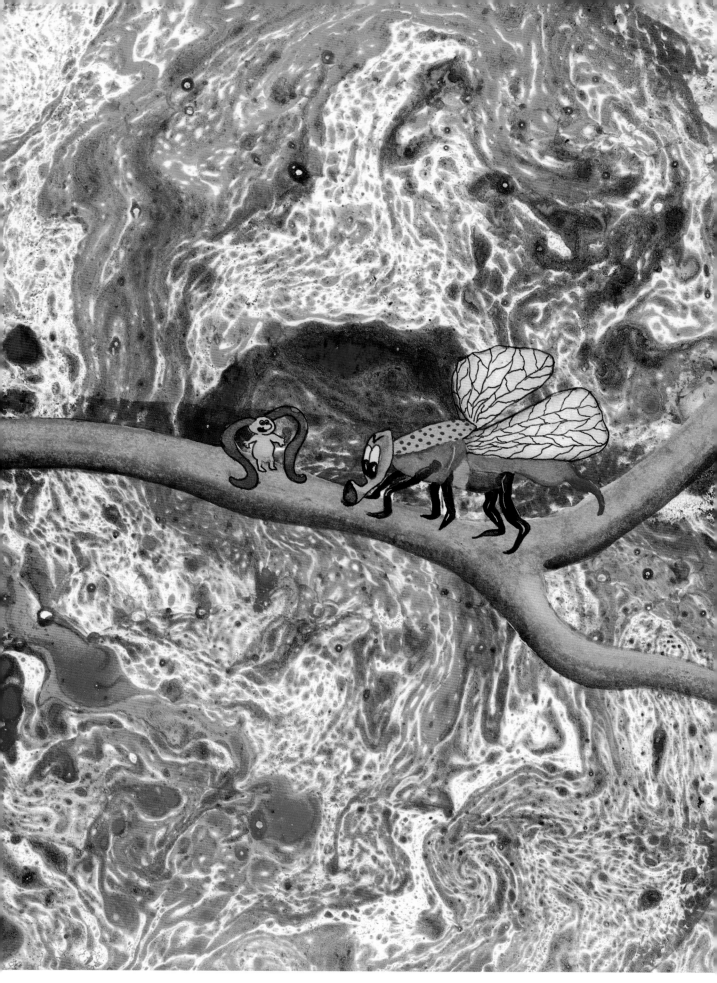

And because he felt like a speck, the tiniest insect in the scrumbly, screechy place wanted to eat him.

So Teenie Weenie went and
hid in a deep, dark hole.

"I feel awful," he said to himself. "What's the point of living in a too hard world? Nothing is good, everything is bad." Then he couldn't be bothered to do anything any more, but stay exactly where he was and be a speck. It was horrible.

Now after a while, along strolled a Wip-Wop bird – the sort that likes looking down deep, dark holes for worms.

To the Wip-Wop bird's surprise, in one particularly deep, dark hole he didn't find a worm, he found a speck. "Hey there, little Speck!" he said to Teenie Weenie, "Why don't you come out of there and have a chocolate muffin in my tree?"

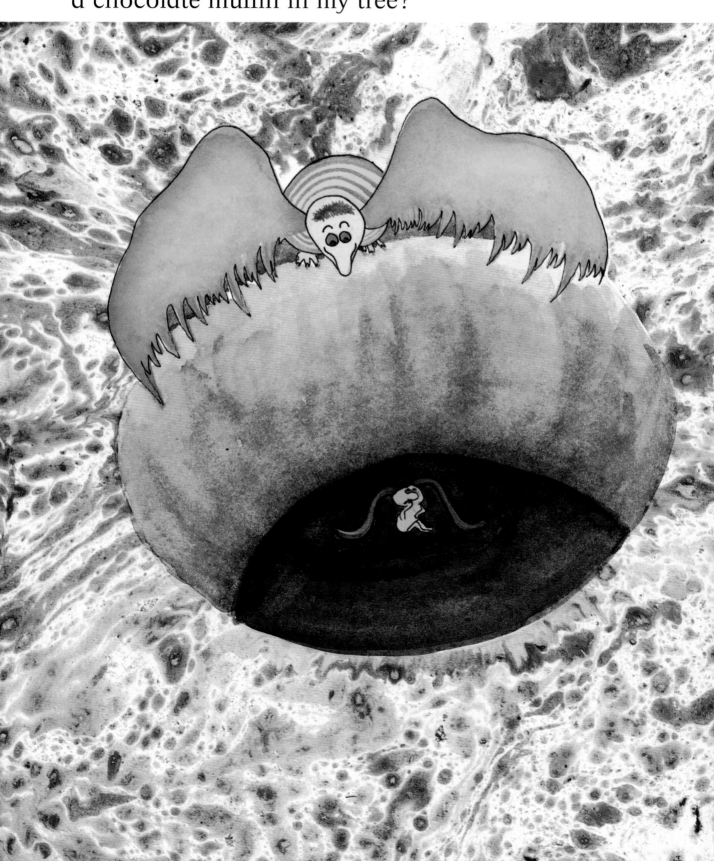

"No, thank you," said Teenie Weenie, in a teenie weenie voice. "It's far too frightening out there in the world."

"Nonsense," said the Wip-Wop bird. "When there's US instead of YOU, it won't be so frightening. I agree that doing too hard things on your own can be far too lonely, but haven't you heard of TOGETHER? Talking of which, here comes my friend Hoggie."

Now, Teenie Weenie didn't know what this TOGETHER thing was, because he'd always done the hard things in his life all by himself, but he decided to give it a go. Anything rather than being a speck. So Teenie Weenie, Hoggie and the Wip-Wop bird set off for chocolate muffins.

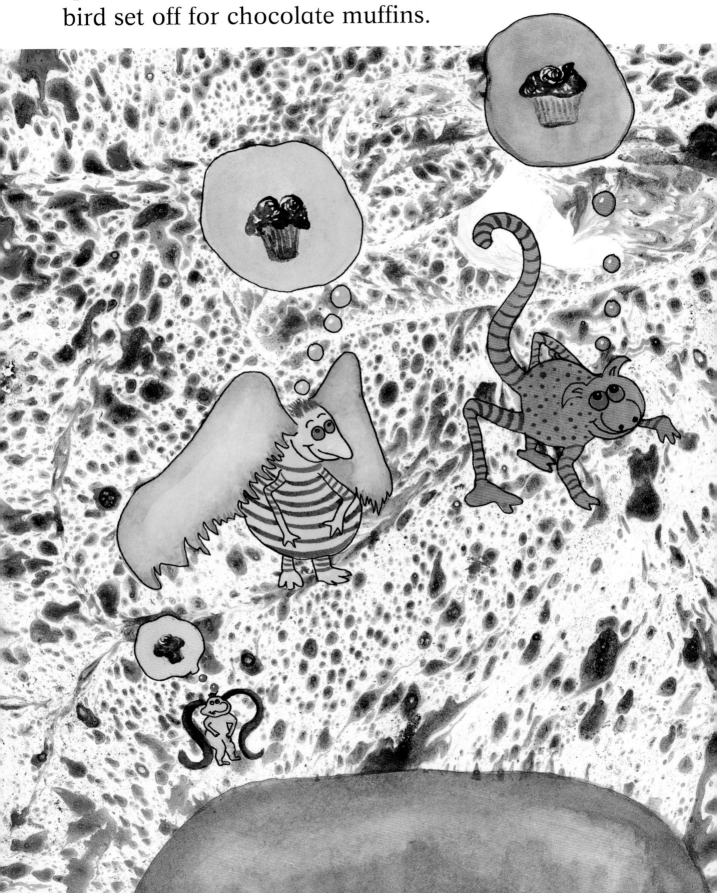

And as they went along, Teenie Weenie started to feel a bit better.

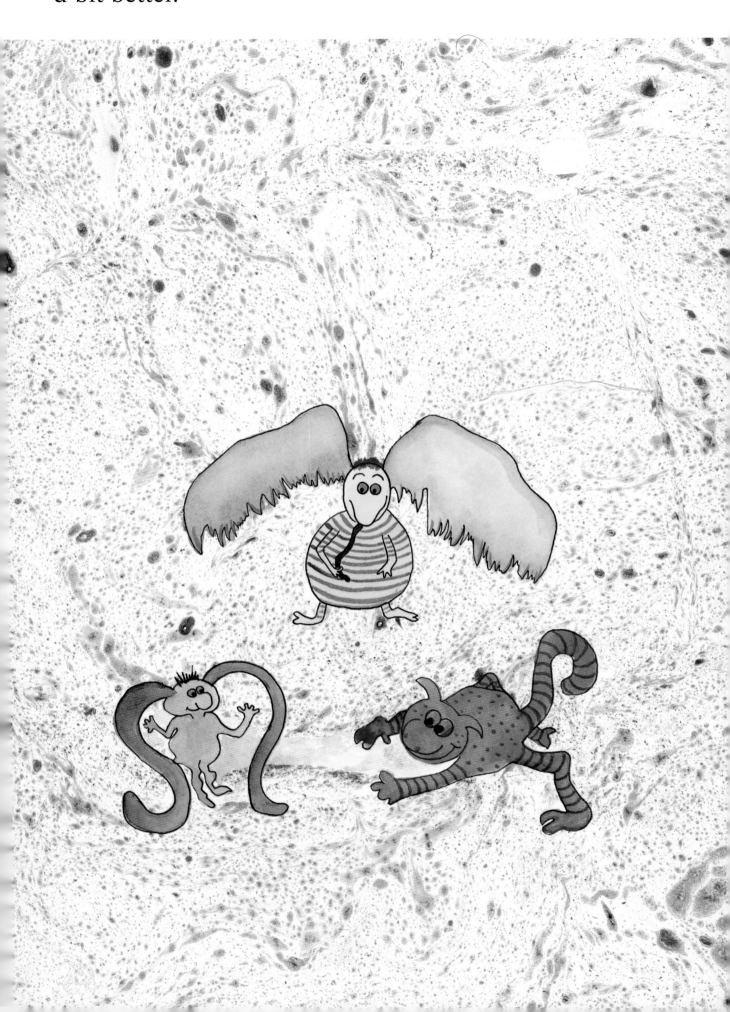

And when they met some Dumping Dits, they all yelled, "Rah!". So the Dits didn't bother them anymore.

And when the Snarling Snippercracker snapped . . .

. . . the Wip-Wop bird, Teenie Weenie and Hoggie
snapped back. "Drat!" said the Snippercracker, "I'll
have to go and do my snarling and my snapping
somewhere else."

And when the big, banging branch tried to whack them, they all shouted, "Stop! You are a bad bullying branch!" And the branch stopped. It's no fun bullying when there's a TOGETHER around.

And when they saw the jangly, tangly mess right there by the water's edge, they sorted it out ever so quickly . . .

. . . and Teenie Weenie even enjoyed the sorting!

Teenie Weenie felt great. Although he was still in the scrumbly, screechy place, it seemed a very different sort of place now that he was not on his own. "You know," he said, "this TOGETHER thing is making me feel all strong and warm inside."

And Teenie Weenie, Hoggie and the Wip-Wop bird ate the lovely muffins, up there in the tall, tall trees.

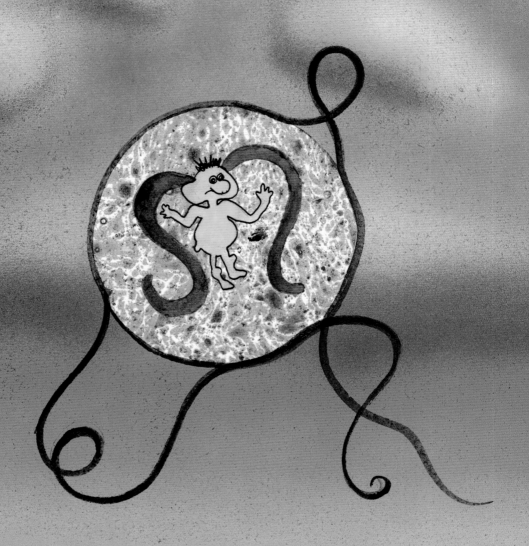

After that, whenever Teenie Weenie found himself starting to shrink, or to lose some of his energy, he said to himself, "Oops! I'm too alone again. I need to do this next bit WITH someone." And off he went to find some TOGETHER.

He never forgot how when things are just too difficult, TOGETHER can feel so good, and ALONE can feel so bad.

And from that time on, Teenie Weenie's life was a far, far better life to live.

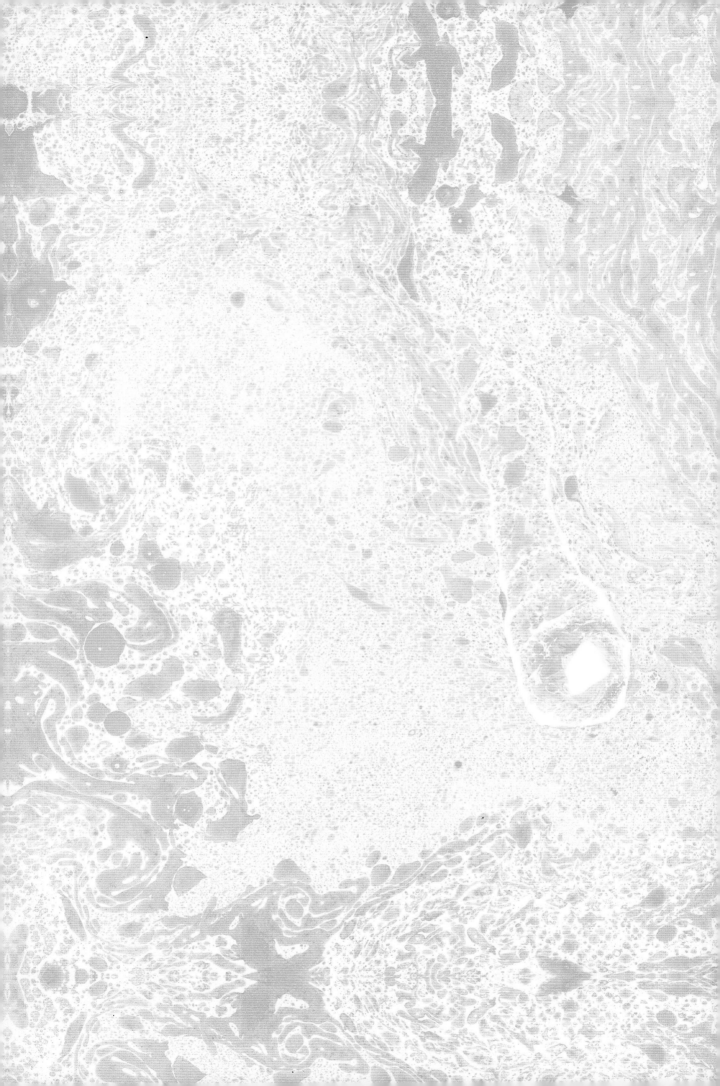